The Little Acorn

Nila Schnirl

Copyright © 2022 Nila Schnirl
All rights reserved
First Edition

NEWMAN SPRINGS PUBLISHING
320 Broad Street
Red Bank, NJ 07701

First originally published by Newman Springs Publishing 2022

ISBN 978-1-68498-172-4 (Paperback)
ISBN 978-1-68498-173-1 (Digital)

Printed in the United States of America

To my family and friends

There once was a little acorn that hung on a tree. He did not want to fall to the ground.

There were three squirrels under the tree, ready to eat or store the acorn if he fell.

So he hung and hung on as long as he could to the tree. The squirrels started up the tree trunk and shook the tree. But the little acorn did not fall.

They were shaking the tree because they were really hungry and wanted to eat the little acorn. They tried and tried to get the little acorn to fall. But he hung on for dear life.

The squirrels were very upset that the little acorn did not fall for them. The squirrels got tired of waiting and left to find food somewhere else.

The little acorn was very happy for this.
He was green and not ripe enough to fall yet.
But he would ripen pretty soon.

The little acorn was so lucky so far. He was out on a thin branch, and no one could get him. They would fall off trying to reach him.

It became spring, and the leaves started to hide him better.
He also worried about birds getting him.

He knew as soon as he was ripe, something would get him and eat him. For sure, he knew it.

All the other acorns had ripened and were already eaten by birds or squirrels.
He was alone and scared.

When night came, the more he came out. He was happy because he was safe at night.

But when daylight came and the sun came out, he was scared again.

He was safe for a while, till the leaves started to fall off. The little acorn would not be hidden anymore. By this time, he would start to turn brown and become ripe soon.

All of a sudden, he saw a big black
bird flying around close to him.
He hung on and stayed very still,
and the big black bird left.
The little acorn was safe again for a while.

He was shaking so bad from the black bird.
The little acorn was afraid he would
drop from all the shaking.
But he was not ripe yet; he was still green.

Night came again, and he was safe for a while.

Daylight came, and the little acorn saw that he was slowly becoming two tones more brown, so he had to start worrying again.

The leaves started to turn colors and fall. The little acorn also knew pretty soon he would fall to the ground and be seen again and maybe eaten.

Well, he was brown now and was ripe. The little acorn fell to the ground; he was so scared being on the ground.

Along came a squirrel who picked up the little acorn.
But the squirrel did not eat him. He buried
the little acorn for another time when
he would be hungry in the winter.
The little acorn was so happy and overjoyed.

So winter came, and the little acorn was still buried and under the snow.
The squirrel came back because he was hungry now. But he could not find where he buried the little acorn because he was hidden under the snow, which made the squirrel really upset.

Little acorn was so happy he was not found or eaten by the squirrel. The little acorn again stayed buried until spring would come.

The snow melted; trees started to bloom again.
All of a sudden, a tree started to
grow. It was the little acorn.

Several winters and summers came and went.
The little acorn grew and grew as time went by.
No one bothered him as he grew bigger. The
little acorn was so surprised by this.

The once-little green acorn turned into
a beautiful oak tree and never was
eaten and lived happy forever.

About the Author

Nila Schnirl is a nurse and one day decided to just sit down and write the book. She likes to try doing new things all the time.

www.ingramcontent.com/pod-product-compliance
Lightning Source LLC
Chambersburg PA
CBHW041436040426
42453CB00019B/2448